Airline Cabin crew English

Intensive
JOB INTERVIEW

Training Module

JORDAN KIM (Chongwook Kim)

Overview
And
Foreword to the Teacher

The Intensive Job Interview Training Module is designed to give the student the competencies needed to succeed in the airline interview.

The study skills and lessons in the module are arranged according to the usual sequence of activities during the airline interview process – pre-interview tests, airline video presentation, group participation exercises, one-on-one interview and panel interview. In each of the interview procedures, the lessons and activities focus on aspects of good communication and performance.

In the Intensive Job Interview Training Module, there are lessons and activities in listening, speaking, reading and writing. Listening and speaking skills are the main foci because these are the most useful in the actual interview itself. However, there are supplemental activities for the development of reading and writing skills, which will come in handy during the pre-interview tests.

The student should be spending a lot of time practicing how to answer specific questions that are commonly asked during actual airline interviews. The teacher should guide the student and give suggestions on how to answer the interview questions correctly in terms of grammar, composition, and diction.

The teacher is asked to exercise her creativity and imagination in the presentation of the lessons and drills, be flexible enough to skip certain exercises if the student has already mastered them, and to supplement the materials, especially the reading selections, with materials relevant to the student's interests and needs.

The student should then be able to apply the lessons and skills that he or she has learned in assessment activities in the form of live, tape-recorded or videotaped sessions.

The culminating activity of the Intensive Job Interview Training is a mock interview with real hiring officers from business process outsourcing companies and other firms that are in the service industries.

TABLE OF CONTENTS

I.   Research and Preparation   **3**

Lesson 1: Asking for information   3
Lesson 2: Making Comparisons   4

II.   Pre-Interview Test   **6**

Lesson 3: Writing about a selected topic   6
Lesson 4: Summarizing a story   7

III.   Company Presentation   **9**

Lesson 5: Listening and taking down notes   9
Lesson 6: Expressing reactions   10
Lesson 7: Asking the right questions   11

IV.   Interaction and Group Participation   **15**

Lesson 8: Going about a group activity   15
Lesson 9: Making suggestions   17
Lesson 10: Expressing pleasure / liking   18

V.   One-on-One Interview   **21**

Lesson 11: Expressing and supporting a personal opinion   21
Lesson 12: Answering questions on personality and career potential   22
Lesson 13: Answering behavioral type of questions   26

VI.   Two-on-One Interview / Panel Interview   **28**

Lesson 14: Reading announcements   29
Lesson 15: Answering scenario-type of questions   30
Lesson 16: Speaking in public   30

VII.   Appendix   **33**

A. Practice Interview Questions and Sample Answers   33
B. Sample Questions for Group Discussion   70
C. Sample Scripts for Practice Interviews   73
D. Sample Curriculum Vitae   75

Research and Preparation

Introduction

The flight attendant interview you will undergo will be much like other job interviews, wherein you need to be professionally dressed, personable and positive throughout the interview. However, competition is expected to be keen because this job usually attracts more applicants than there are available jobs, with only the most qualified eventually being hired, so preparation is important. Besides, true professionalism requires forethought and planning.

Skills Development

- Asking for information
- Noting and selecting significant details
- Drawing conclusions and inferences

Lesson 1: Asking for information

Obtaining information about job fairs and vacancies is the first step to starting a career of your choice. Knowing as much information as you can about the company that has an opening would certainly give you an advantage.

Go to their website and learn several facts about them, such as any new routes they may be planning, if they have ordered any new airplanes, how many flight attendants they plan to hire this year, or changes in management such as the name of their new Operations Manager or CEO.

You also need to have a good understanding of the life of a flight attendant. Ask a flight attendant to learn about his or her job and lifestyle.

The following italicized expressions would be useful when gathering information:
Have you read (or heard) about an opening for flight attendants?
Please tell me about Philippine Airlines.
I'm interested in becoming a flight attendant. *Can you tell me* how it's like?

ACTIVITY: DOING YOUR RESEARCH

Choose an airline or company that you want to apply with and find out about the company and the position: job location, pay and benefits, financial data, work schedule, duties and responsibilities. Prepare your questions beforehand and submit to your teacher for correction. Make a report on your little research.

Lesson 2: Making comparisons

While job hunting, there are instances when we compare one position from another, one company from the other. In certain instances, we say what a company is not, *in contrast* to what is familiar to us.

When writing a paragraph of *comparison* and *contrast*, you describe a person, a career, or situation first, in its entirety, then the other.

Example: *Before we had the Light Rail Transit, the commuters had to endure the heat and the dust as they waited for long hours inside the jeepney or buses plying between Pasay City and Quezon City.*

ACTIVITY: WRITING A PARAGRAPH OF COMPARISON
Write a paragraph comparing and contrasting one of the following:

1. Becoming a flight attendant or taking on a different career
2. Ready-to-cook food and home-made meals
3. High school and college life

Do's and Don'ts

- Obtain as much information as you can about the airline where you will be interviewing. It will be most uncomfortable for you if you have to admit that you know little or nothing about the airline. It will be to your advantage if you can intelligently discuss details of the airline's operations, history, etc.

- Keep abreast of all the information and latest happening pertaining to the airline. Questions pertaining to latest news concerning the airline can be asked to judge your background knowledge as well as interest in the field. A good source for such information is the airline website; it generally has the history and latest news concerning the company.

- You should be updated on current affairs and news relating to the aviation industry.

- Before your interview, you should go through your life's timeline, trying to remember experiences that stand out in your mind. Then write down the ones that you feel would relate to the flight attendant position.

- When confirming an appointment for an interview by phone, do not ask how to find the station or where to park. To ask such questions is to give the impression that you can't find your way around.

- Before going to another town for a job interview, take time to learn something about that community.

Assessing Your Potential

SELF-ASSESSMENT CHECKLIST:

✓ Is my physical appearance appropriate to the kind of position I seek?

✓ If it is not, can my appearance be made acceptable or adequate through hair styling, make-up, and so forth?

✓ Do I have a personality that is engaging and unique?

✓ What is there about me that makes me feel that I can succeed as a flight attendant?

Enriching Your Skills

Answer the following questions and submit your answers to your teacher for correction:

1) Would you please tell me your name?
   (May I have your name, please?)

   _____

2) What is your family name?
   (What is your last name?)
   (What's your surname)?

   My family name is Choi. (Kim, Lee, Park)

   Your answer:

   _____

3) May I ask your present address?
   (Where do you live now?)

   _____

4) What is your home address?
   My home address is 124-56 Yonsan-dong, Dongrae-gu, and Busan.

   _____

5) What is your current occupation?

   _____

Pre – Interview Test

Introduction

At most airlines, you can expect to take a series of aptitude tests. Some of these are very similar to the Scholastic Aptitude Test. You can be tested on a variety of subjects, including basic math, reading comprehension, spelling and analogies. Hence, proficiency in reading and writing is needed.

At the Open Session, typically you will be asked to fill out a questionnaire and will be given a short speech about the airline by a flight attendant representative. Each person may then be required to take a written, multiple-choice test, which includes some customer service questions. Beyond aptitude tests, you might also be given motor skills and/or psychological tests. Those that pass the test will be asked to remain while the others are excused.

While these tests and assessments are all an attempt at standardization and greater objectivity, they are all lacking to a certain degree. They still have a subjective element. Be prepared, both mentally and physically, for these tests and assessments.

Skills Development

- Writing about a selected topic
- Answering guide questions
- Summarizing significant details

Lesson 3: Writing about a selected topic

By this time you probably know already that a paragraph is composed of sentences, which work as a team and fit together. A paragraph has a main idea and all the sentences in that paragraph must relate to that main idea.

One of the most effective ways of organizing written or spoken material is to write or talk around a main idea and support it with data – facts, arguments, examples, or details, which will make the reader accept the main idea as true. The main idea may be stated at the beginning, at the middle or at the end of the paragraph.

EXERCISE: WRITING

Write a short paragraph about a place you have seen, read or heard about. Read the paragraph in front of a group of people.

Lesson 4: Summary Writing

A summary gives the main idea of a longer piece of writing or video presentation in a very compact form, but without, in any way, modifying or changing the writer's tone or point of view.

The following steps are to be followed in writing a summary:
1. Read the selection carefully.
2. Look for the main ideas.
3. Study how the ideas were developed step by step.
4. Use your own words, limiting your number of words to one-third or one-fourth of the original piece.
5. Stick as closely as you can to the plan of ideas of the original piece when you write your summary.

EXERCISE: WRITING A SUMMARY

1. Write a brief summary on the following passage:

In order that life may have meaning, it has to be spent for God and for others. To live only for one's self is to live a life without meaning. Sooner or later, one realizes that one's life is but an empty shell because one has not really loved. On the other hand, if life has to have a meaning, it has to be spent for others. This is because man is made to live with others. This is because man is a social being. In the final analysis our meaning in life lies on how much we have contributed to the happiness, welfare and well-being of others. And in order that our giving of ourselves to our fellowmen be in the right track and not off-track, we need to give ourselves to God.

2. Ask someone who has not read the original text to read the summary. If he understood it, then you have written a good summary.

3. Read a news feature, a magazine article or any selection specified by the teacher. Summarize the article or selection in no more than two paragraphs.

Dos and Don'ts

- Many of the tests during the airline interview are timed. If you have had a great deal of success on standardized tests, you should not worry. On the other hand, if these types of tests tend to trouble you, you should pick up an aptitude test preparation guide for assistance.

- You should be updated on current affairs and news relating to the aviation industry.

- Do not misrepresent yourself or your abilities in any way.

Assessing Your Potential
SELF-ASSESSMENT CHECKLIST:

✓ Have I properly prepared myself to work as a flight attendant?
✓ Am I willing to spend years of frequent travel, often being away from family and friends for weeks at a time?
✓ Am I prepared to move anywhere at any time to further my career?

Enriching Your Skills
Answer the following questions and submit your answers to your teacher.

1) How big is your family?
   (How many are there in your family?)

   There are six members in my family. They are my parents, elder brother, a younger brother, a younger sister and myself.

   _____

   _____

   _____

2) Do you have any children?
   (Do you have any kids?)

   a) *Yes, I gave birth to a baby boy last month.*

   b) *No, I don't. I'm still single.*

3) What do your parents say about your decision to become a flight attendant?

My parents are very supportive of what I do.

_____

_____

4) Who do you want to be as your roommate among your colleagues of different nationalities?
(Which nationality do you prefer to live with as a flat mate? Give your reason.

I don't mind what nationality. I'm not so picky about whom to have as a roommate, although I'd rather that we'd be of the same gender.

_____

_____

_____

_____

_____

5) Have you ever been ill?
(Have you ever been sick?)

No, I haven't. I am quite healthy.

When I was in second year high school, I was hospitalized for an appendectomy. Since then I haven't had any other trip to the doctor.

Company Presentation

Introduction

Oftentimes, during the interview process, you will also receive an overview of the company and the job description from a representative of the airline.

You will also be required to take a video test. Typically, several vignettes are shown on videotape that features flight attendants who are forced to handle difficult in-flight situations. Your job, after watching each clip, is to critique the way each flight attendant handles the particular situation. You will need to respond using your own judgment.

Skills Development

- Listening to get main ideas and supporting details
- Expressing reactions
- Asking the right questions

Lesson 5: Listening and taking down notes

When you are shown audio – visual reference materials to know more about the airline, listen well to the video presentation or briefing / orientation. Jot down notes if you think you cannot trust your memory.

You can make the most of any reference material if you first understand the main idea and its supporting details. Make brief notes of these main points and details. You form a paragraph for each idea or note down sentences that contain important information or do an outline.

ACTIVITY / EXERCISE: LISTENING TO A COMPANY BRIEF

Work with your class partner and take turns being the pretend airline representative then being pretend flight attendant applicant.   The pretend airline representative gives a short speech about the airline and the pretend flight attendant listens and takes down notes. Each student will then be required to take a written test based on the respective company brief that was given.

Lesson 6: Expressing reactions

In a job interview, you will be asked to express your reactions or attitudes to things, events and people around. In expressing reactions and attitudes, you will find this list of words useful:

impress	attract	upset	offend
excite	irritate	surprise	embarrass
interest	confuse	astonish	terrify
shock	amuse	fascinate	admire

Example:
Mario: What do you think of travelling?
Mila: Oh, it's <u>exciting</u>.
Mario: Yes, travelling is really exciting. And fascinating, too

Sometimes instead of using the adjective form of the verbs as in the preceding exchange, verbs are used as in the following:

I admire _____.
_____ get on my nerves.
I can't stand _____.
I hate _____.
I like _____.

Example:
Helen: What things annoy you?
Nancy: I can't stand people who are presumptuous.
Helen: Me, too.
Nancy: Something else often gets on my nerves.
Helen: What's that?
Nancy: I hate people who are dishonest.

ACTIVITY: LISTENING AND REACTING

After watching a videotaped speech of a keynote speaker or watching a short documentary film or video, express your reactions by answering the following questions:

What ideas in the speech / documentary particularly ...
   a. impress you?
   b. fascinate you?
   c. interest you?
   d. depress you?

Lesson 7: Asking the right questions

An interview is the first step towards success. The only problem is that many interviewees end up making costly mistakes during their interviews. One of those mistakes is by not asking any questions. You are advised against doing this. Not asking any questions during a job interview gives the impression that you are not a leader, just a follower. That is not the type of impression that you want to make.

Some questions can throw up answers that can be another question for you from the recruitment team, so be careful while putting forth questions. Questions must be relevant to the company and the job. Avoid asking questions on issues that have been covered during any presentations given to you by the recruitment team.

When it comes to asking questions during a job interview, you may be wondering what type of questions you should ask. Before examining the type of questions that you should ask, it may be best to focus on the type of questions that you shouldn't ask. For one, you are advised against asking about the pay or raises, like when they kick in. Salary is something that should be brought up by the interviewer. If and when salary is discussed, you may want to ask about raises, but it is advised that you refrain from doing so, at least right away.

In keeping with questions that you should not ask, many employers give their job applicants information about their company, like a company brochure or a link to their online

website. You are advised to thoroughly examine all of the information given to you, whether that information be online or in print. This will prevent you from asking questions that you should already know the answers to. Asking a question about the history of the company, when you were already given detailed history information gives the impression that you did not read through the materials given to you. This is not the type of first impression that you want to make.

Now that you know some of the questions that you do not want to ask during a job interview, you may want to focus on some of the questions that you can ask or at least ones that are considered safe, to ask. One of those questions is about the average workday or workweek. For instance, ask if you were hired for the job, what would your workdays or workweeks be like? What type of tasks would you be required to complete?

Another question that you may want to ask during a job interview is about the company's future. Are there any plans for expansion? How does the company rate against the competition? These are interesting questions that show that you want to work for a successful company, one that will be around for a long period of time. Asking about the stability of a company gives a good impression of yourself, as it often means that you are also looking for stability.

The above mentioned questions are just a few of the many that you may want to ask an interviewer during a job interview. In all honesty, you are advised to use your best judgment when asking questions, but it is important that you do ask at least some.

EXERCISE: FORMULATING QUESTIONS

Remember the company research you made in Activity 1? Based on the information you gathered from that little research, formulate at least five questions about the company that you might want to ask the airline representatives during your interview. Submit those questions to your teacher for corrections in grammar and sentence construction.

Dos and Don'ts

- Do prepare fully for your interview.
- Do feel comfortable with your clothes but be smart and businesslike.
- Be early.
- Make a list of the questions you would like to ask.
- Make yourself at home and be friendly with everyone. Do smile and be polite to everyone you meet.
- Talk to everyone but do not be overpowering.
- After the company brief or video, think of a great question. They note that in your application.
- Do think positive and relax.
- Don't be rude or offhand to anyone you meet.
- Don't make critical comments about former employers.
- Don't tell lies as you'll nearly always be found out.
- Don't underplay your achievements, sell yourself.
- Don't panic.
- Finally, thank your interviewer for their time, smile and give them a firm handshake.

Assessing Your Potential

SELF-ASSESSMENT CHECKLIST:

- ✓ Do I have the ability to speak clearly?
- ✓ Do I have excellent health?
- ✓ Do I have a genuine outgoing personality?

Enriching Your Skills

Answer the following questions. Elaborate on your answers.

1) What do you know about our company?

_____

_____

_____

2) Why do you want to work for our airline?
   (Why did you apply to this airline?)
   (Tell me the reasons why you'd like to work for our company.)
   (Why are you interested in our company?)

   (TIP: Do your homework and research the airline. Each airline has a different emphasis. Your answer should focus on what appeals to you about the airline and how you fit with their emphasis.)

   I learned that your airline has a good reputation in terms of service excellence, safe working conditions, career advancement, and benefits. That's the kind of company that I would like to be part of, the kind of company where I could use my skills and personality to the fullest.

   I'd like to grow with a successful company.

_____

_____

_____

_____

3) Why do you like to be a flight attendant?

I know a flight attendant's job is all about service. However, compared to other service-oriented jobs, a flight attendant gets more rewards while on the job. She gets to meet a lot of people, including celebrities, see new places, and get paid for it. I don't think I would find that kind of opportunity in a 9-to-5 job.

_____

_____

_____

_____

_____

4) What makes you think you would be a good flight attendant?

I have a naturally friendly, positive communication style. I could very well use this trait if I become a flight attendant for your airline.

_____

_____

_____

_____

5) How do you react to insinuations that flight attendants are in the real sense just waitresses in fabulous uniforms?

_____

_____

_____

_____

Interaction and Group Participation

Introduction

What sets an airline interview apart from other job interviews is that at your airline interview, aside from the fact that you will be assessed in areas of appearance and customer service work history, you will also be evaluated in terms of your abilities to interact with others, your understanding of customer service, and your overall personality. It is imperative for a would-be flight attendant to understand that it is not just personality that counts but also presence of mind, a good command of English (English being the International Aviation Language) and a great deal of stamina.

Airline interviews will generally require you to take part in a group exercise, to let the airline see how you work with others on a task.

Airlines prefer to hire poised, tactful, and resourceful people who can interact comfortably with strangers and remain calm under duress, pleasant, and efficient regardless of how tired they are or how demanding passengers may be.

Skills Development

- Making suggestions
- Interacting with others
- Comprehending phrases and sentence meaning

Lesson 8: Going about a group activity

The group activity within an airline interview procedure is all about participation and listening skills. If you sit back and be shy, you will not go any farther with the interview process.

What happens in a team exercise or group activity is something like this... They call groups of about 5 - 10 people. They take them to a conference room or a similar venue. Then they give the group some tasks to accomplish as a group under time pressure.

The secret to the team exercise is that there is no right or wrong. Only that you participate in the exercise. Use your group member's first names. They all have name tags.

If the airline people tell you to be discreet, do not say anything even if someone asked how your interview went. Just say they told us not to talk about it. People posing as applicants could be put in the room to be the eyes and ears. This little game happens in most airlines.

During the team exercise, just remember this: participate and follow instructions.

EXERCISE: ANSWERING QUESTIONS ON TEAMWORK

Answer the following questions on interaction and teamwork. Elaborate on each answer.

1) Do you work well with others?

Yes, I get along well with other people. I'd say I am a team player.

_____

_____

2) Are you a sociable person or a loner?

I am sociable because I enjoy being with other people.

_____

_____

3) Why do you want to change your current company and role?

I have always been fascinated with traveling and going places. I thought the only way to fulfill those dreams within my capacity would be to become a flight attendant. It would be like going on a vacation while working. Besides, I have been working on a regular 8 to 5 job that has become less challenging after several years. I think it's time for a change.

_____

_____

_____

_____

_____

4) How do your friends describe you as a person?

My friends say I'm honest and diligent. I always try to do my best in accomplishing the tasks that are given to me. I am not comfortable about leaving something half-done.

_____

_____

_____

_____

_____

5) What do you enjoy most about working as part of a team?

I like listening to the exchange of ideas and seeing the cooperation of the team members. The best part of a team activity is the feeling you get after completing the task that has been assigned to your team.

_____

_____

_____

_____

_____

Lesson 9: Making suggestions

Participating in a team exercise or a group activity during an airline interview presents a window of opportunity to show the airline people how well you get along with others and how you manage the task given to you or the team. In the team exercise, you have to be a team player. When you have an idea that could make things work faster, do not dictate your idea to the group; instead, you make a suggestion.

When making suggestions, you can use any of the following expressions:

Why don't you (or we)...	*do this?*
Why not ...	*listen to my idea?*
I suggest that you try to...	

ACTIVITY:

With a partner or a group, perform any of the following group activities:

1. Plan or make a program for a volunteer activity.

2. Make a travel itinerary for a group of 20 people who are disabled or handicapped.

3. Think of an item or product and create an advertisement within 15 minutes. Then you or any representative of your group will advertise the product in front of the class.

Lesson 10: Expressing Pleasure/Liking

There are times when you hear, see read, or observe things that you like. You express your joy or pleasure by saying expressions like the following:

That's a	*nice*	*way of*	*saying it.*
	beautiful		*putting it.*
	thoughtful		*doing it.*
That's	*beautifully*		*done.*
	sensitively		*expressed.*
	nicely		*said.*

When you do not like what has been done, you express your displeasure or disliking by saying expressions like the following:

That's not a	*nice*	*thing*	*to say.*
	beautiful		*to do.*
	thoughtful		*to do.*

EXERCISE: GROUP DISCUSSION

Form a small group. Tackle the following topics of discussion and report the thoughts of the group to the teacher.

1)   Give positive natural facts and negative natural facts about Koreans.

2)   Talk about three national or global issues prevailing in Korea at this time.

3)   Give three positive and three negative things about the Korean educational system.

Dos and Don'ts

- Carry a warm disposition, a welcoming behavior and great appearance, as they are crucial in creating the right impression in the mind of the interviewer.
- Befriend other candidates and try to remember their names as there can be some questions about them from the interviewer to know about your interpersonal skills, as the flight attendant's job is more of teamwork.
- Remember to address people in a friendly and well-mannered way.
- Be yourself in the interview and never try to be someone you are not. Recruitment personnel are highly trained and will spot anyone who tries to impress.
- Ensure that you are open to suggestions and queries by all team members, and that you participate in all discussions and exercises.
- Never be aggressive and imposing. Do not be overpowering, but participate.

Assessing Your Potential

SELF-ASSESSMENT CHECKLIST:

- ✓ Can I perform effectively under pressure?
- ✓ Do I possess the manipulative skills necessary to become an efficient flight attendant?
- ✓ Do I take direction well, responding quickly and sensitively to instructions?

Enriching Your Skills

Answer the following questions. Support your answers with specific details from experiences.

1) Do you do things better and faster by yourself or with others?

   Of course, I do things faster by myself but not necessarily better. Sometimes working with others would produce better results.

   _____

   _____

   _____

   _____

2) Are you more of a follower or a leader?

   a) *They say a good leader is a good follower. And I believe that. I am ready to follow a leader who has the best ideas and knows what's best for the team. On the other hand, I am ready to take charge if it's necessary.*

   b) *I don't try to get in front of people and lead them. I would rather cooperate with everybody else, and get the job done by working together.*

   c) *I don't agree with someone else's opinion right away but if I see his point and it's good, then I would no longer have any second thoughts about cooperating.*

   _____

   _____

   _____

   _____

   _____

3) Describe your personality.

   a) *My personality is what I would call outgoing. I like to be in the company of other people. There is so much to learn from them. I am the type of person with a very positive approach to things and life in general.*

   b) *I am a focused person. I don't like to leave anything half-done. It makes me nervous. I couldn't concentrate on something else until the first thing is finished.*

   _____

   _____

   _____

   _____

4) A flight attendant must deal with all kinds of people and remain courteous. Do you have a lot of patience with other people?

   I have a wide understanding of people's behavior. I do not become frustrated easily if I encounter a difficult passenger.

   _____

   _____

   _____

   _____

5) Can you do multi-tasking?

   Yes, I can do several tasks and get them done on schedule. I am very good at time management and organization.

   _____

   _____

   _____

One-on-One Interview

Introduction

The interview procedure commonly starts with the initial interview, where they pare down the potential applicants from the rest. This is more of a personality check.

The one-on-one interview is the most common type of interview during the flight attendant employment process. Depending on the airline, it could be your first or last interview; in some cases, a one-on-one may be the only type of interview you have to experience.

The primary focus of the questions will be to see how much you understand about customer service.

Skills Development

- Expressing and supporting an opinion
- Answering questions based on real life experiences

Lesson 11: Expressing and supporting an opinion

When you wish to say something that you personally believe in, you express a personal point of view. To do this, you may say:

In my opinion ...
Personally, I think...
As far as I'm concerned...
I'd like to point out that...

You may agree or disagree with someone else's point of view. When you agree, you may use some of the following expressions:

Exactly! You hit the nail right on the head.
I think so, too.
I go along with that.
You're right.

When you disagree, you may use some of the following expressions:
On the contrary...
I'm sorry to disagree...

Keep in mind these pointers when giving opinions to issues that may be brought up during airline interviews:

Support your views. Don't stop with "I think this way because I want to." Give reasons and motives for your opinions. Draw on personal experience backed up by some satisfactory authority. Avoid hearsay and generalizations.

Stick to matters that are open to full discussion. Avoid judging people, foolish criticism and gossip.

Be courteous. Learn to listen and respect opinions different from yours.

ACTIVITY: GROUP DISCUSSION

Form small groups and give your opinion on one of the topics that follow. The members of the group may express their agreement or disagreement. Remember to be courteous to the rest of your group even as you express disagreement.

- The responsibility of a leader is very hard.
- Authority and power make a man forget himself.
- English has influences on our future.
- Pick three things in Korean culture, which you are proud of and three things that you think need to be improved.

Lesson 12: Answering questions on personality and career potential

Prior to the interview, you should already be thinking about the questions you might be asked and how you will respond to them. Most interviewers will ask some similar basic questions. Some typical questions are:

- What are your strengths and weaknesses?
- What are the main responsibilities in your current role?
- What do you most enjoy about your current role?
- What do you enjoy most about working as part of a team?
- Can you describe a time when you've faced a difficult challenge and how you overcame it?
- What interested you in this position?
- What skills could you bring to this position?
- Why do you want to change your current company and role?

However, the most common and most ramble-prone question of all is "Tell me about yourself." This is often the first question asked after the initial introductions and small talk and is therefore critical to creating a good first impression. It is also an opportunity for you to deliver a knockout answer that helps to build your confidence for the rest of the interview.

To answer this question effectively, concentrate on your important achievements, spare the details. Experienced interviewers are generally more interested in how you approach your answer than any specific detail.

Your answer to the question should <u>not be longer than 5 minutes</u>:
1 minute (maximum) for your personal history
1 minute for your educational background, and
3 minutes (maximum) for your career background.

Personal history might include where you were born and raised, family background and any other interesting points. When giving an overview of your personal history it is acceptable to reveal a little bit about yourself. For example to share some insight into your childhood. This will demonstrate your openness to the interviewer and will help to build rapport.

Educational background should highlight your academic achievements. Start with your resume. Review the section that lists your academic achievements and qualifications. Write down the two or three achievements you are most proud of during your periods of study. Examples might be academic results, participation in student groups, or your ability to juggle full time work and part time study commitments.

Career background should include your professional experience and skills. Try to pick out the most notable achievements for yourself and the teams you have worked with. Make sure you describe your own contribution to the achievement, and wherever possible the effect it had on the organization. Ideally, you will have at least one achievement noted for each of your three most recent roles.

With your academic and career achievements written down it is time to practice verbally delivering your answer. Continue to practice until you are comfortable with both the content and the structure of your answer. This question is so crucial to the success of your interview that it is <u>worth spending 20% of your overall interview preparation time on</u>.

EXERCISE: ANSWERING QUESTIONS ON PERSONALITY AND CAREER POTENTIAL

Answer the following questions. Elaborate on each answer.

1) Tell me the reasons why you want to work for this company.

   Your company offers good opportunities for career development. I've heard about how flight attendants in your airline are enjoying a rewarding career. I would like to be one of them. I could use my four-year experience in customer service in this job.

   _____

   _____

   _____

2) This job requires that you travel frequently. Will that fit in with your lifestyle and family plans?

   I'm single and I have spent a lot of time overseas already, so you can be sure that I have no problems with frequent trips abroad.

   When I applied for this job, I was aware that traveling would be required. I discussed this with my wife, and she understood that this job presents a good opportunity for me. We both agreed that the frequent trips would not be a problem.

   _____

   _____

   _____

3) What are your strengths and weaknesses?

   My strength lies in my ability to easily adapt to a new environment or new people around me. I don't have a problem about adjusting to changes in my life. I'm thinking like "What's the use of resisting to change?" That would be a waste of time and effort. I'd rather look at change as new possibilities or an opportunity to grow...That attitude is probably my weakness, too. Because I just go with the flow, to some people I come across as a happy-go-lucky person.

_____

_____

_____

_____

4) What skills could you bring to this position?

I have good intuition and perception to sense the needs, talents and abilities of other people that could be put to use especially in problematic situations. These are skills that relate to the job that I am applying for.

_____

_____

_____

_____

_____

5) Are you a responsible person?

People tell me I have a strong sense of responsibility because I go beyond what is expected of me to get things done. However, I tend to be a perfectionist, which other people may consider a weakness although I consider it as another strong point because it sets a high standard in everything I do.

_____

_____

_____

_____

_____

ACTIVITY: PRACTICE INTERVIEW (Tape-recorded Session)

Answer the question "Tell me about yourself" keeping in mind the technique and structure you learned in Lesson 12. Record your 3-minute answer on an audio recorder. You also tape your answers to the questions on personality and career potential in the previous exercise. Let your teacher evaluate your delivery.

Using an audio recorder has numerous advantages, like you do not need anyone else to help you. You can dictate your response to each question and then play them back for analysis. Be particularly attentive to your use of what we call "useless words," such as "You know," "Ya know," "like," etc. These words have no place in an interview setting. You can also try to record the interview with a friend asking the questions. Here again, you can benefit from someone else's feedback.

Lesson 13: Answering behavioral type of questions

There are many types of interview questions, but one of the most common types now being used at most interviews is the "Behavioral Question."

A behavioral question is one that asks you about a past experience. Human resource managers and flight attendant recruiters feel that one's actions in handling past experiences can be a good measure of future success.

The behavioral question is usually a three-part question. The first part asks about the specific experience; the second asks how you handled it; and the third part asks for the outcome.

When you are put forth a question such as "Tell me why I should select you," it is your job to give a persuasive answer to hire you based on your qualifications. Blow your own trumpet – this is a chance to sell yourself to the company. Give them a good reason to hire your services - impress upon them how reliable, punctual, flexible you are, how you are able to anticipate the needs of others, an essential requirement of any customer service job. Communicate how your positive contributions and performance at your present job will relate to that of the flight attendant position.

When asked, "Why do you want to be a flight attendant?" be different and creative. Do NOT say that oft repeated run of the mill answer like you want to travel and you like to meet people – that's the most common answer, and they would have heard that hundreds of times a day! Give an answer that implies that you enjoy giving good customer service, or that it's like going to work every day and feeling like you're on vacation; emphasize your passion for flying since that is what you will be actually doing in a flight attendant job, and be creative with your answer! Really dig into what it is that appeals to you about the job, and think about what it is that charms you to the position.

For the question "Why do you want to work for this airline?" you first need to know and establish the fact that you already know something about the airline. Then you want to convince them what difference you could bring to their company, giving specific examples of how the company has already influenced your life or how it will in the future. Keep in mind that this is your big chance to persuade them to hire you, so learn all you can about how

your background will help you fit into their company's culture, and don't be afraid to flaunt your accomplishments and assets!

ACTIVITY: PRACTICE INTERVIEW (live-session)

Here are a few examples of behavioral questions that you may encounter in an interview. Answer them first on paper and then orally before a live audience. Each answer should not be more than 5 minutes.

1. Give an example of a situation where you had to deal with a disgruntled customer and the outcome.

2. Give an example of a situation where your family did not support you and how you handled it.

3. Give an example of a situation where you had to go the extra mile to please somebody.

Dos and Don'ts

- Always be polite and friendly to everyone you see in the offices, and if appropriate, make conversation with them. When you enter a room, stand up straight, smile and give your interviewer a firm handshake.
- Be yourself. Do not try to act the part of the person you assume the interviewer is looking for.
- Match your eye contact with that of the interviewer. Most interviewers maintain strong eye contact, but if you meet one who does not, act accordingly. If the interviewer looks you in the eye, try to reciprocate. Take your cue from him or her.
- If you can't answer a question because you don't have the relevant experience, try to give an answer that is as close as you can to what they are looking for.
- Be prepared to tell your life story – in an abbreviated form, of course. This might include where you were born, where you grew up, schools attended, significant travel, relevant job experience, and where you are headed in your career.
- It is usually a good policy to be honest at any airline interview. But do not go into specifics about leaving your former employer/company unless specifically asked by an interviewer. Some may leave for a variety of reasons including family illness, divorce, childcare issues, etc. The only way the hiring airline would have specific information about the resignation is if a supervisor or manager is given as a reference and that person is contacted directly. Even then, the issue may not come up.
- Do not feel the need to mention every detail of your education and career. Instead, focus on your achievements.
- Do not take chances by making small talk that might reveal ignorance. Do not venture opinions about the airline industry in general unless they are completely to the point of the interview.
- Do not try to entertain by taking over the interview and telling stories, anecdotes, or jokes.

Assessing Your Potential

During a flight attendant interview, there are a number of factors that can effectively qualify you for consideration. If you measure up to this yardstick, you are on your way to a successful interview.

SELF-ASSESSMENT CHECKLIST:

- ✓ Is my personal appearance up to the desired standards?
- ✓ Do I have purpose and goals in life?
- ✓ Am I enthusiastic – not passive or indifferent?
- ✓ Am I able to relate experience-based examples when answering behavioral-type questions?
- ✓ Do I know how to ask the right questions at the appropriate time?
- ✓ Do I have a vast knowledge about the airline and the duties and responsibilities of a flight attendant?
- ✓ Am I prepared?

Enriching Your Skills

By far, the best and the most economical way to practice interviewing is to have a friend or teacher to conduct mock interview sessions. The mock interview sessions should be set up in a part of your home or school to replicate exactly the interviewing environment - perhaps an office with a desk, so you can incorporate as much realism as possible into the interview practice session. The "interviewer" should ask you the questions provided below and critique your responses, body language, etc. If you are preparing for an open interview, practice answering these questions in front of a large group of friends or family members and ask for their feedback.

- What are the main responsibilities in your current role?
- What do you most enjoy about your current role?
- Can you describe a time when you've faced a difficult challenge and how you overcame it?
- What interested you in this position?
- Tell us about a situation that you have experienced where you demonstrated your ability to make good decisions under pressure.
- If there were no rules in your life for one day and you could be outrageous, what would you do?
- Tell me some of your recent goals and what you did to achieve them.
- If you had to live your life over again, what is the one thing you would change?

Two-on-One and Group Interviews

Introduction

During a two-on-one and group interviews, you will have to direct your attention to two people rather than one. The two-on-one interview may take place the same day as the one-on-one or it could take place at a later date. During a two-on-one or panel interview, you will be asked more specific questions than in the pre-interview and it will generally take a great deal longer. If the airline calls you for a return interview, you have passed the most difficult part of the flight attendant employment process.

Basically, the interviewers are looking for good listening skills, good eye contact with other candidates, an ability to speak clearly and without hesitation, body language and poise that projects a good image of the airline.

Skills Development

- Speaking audibly in public
- Answering interview questions correctly

Lesson 14: Reading announcements

Part of a flight attendant's job is to read in-flight announcements. Your goal is to communicate the message or messages effectively to the passengers. For some, the ability to communicate comes easily. For most, however, difficulty in being effective even in daily conversation is a reminder that much work lies ahead.

True communication begins when you reflect yourself in your delivery and realize that you are speaking to individuals, not to a crowd.

It is your responsibility to ensure that the ideas of the announcement are clearly transmitted to the minds of the passengers. Of course, you can achieve this purpose only if you do not misread or mispronounce words. Beyond this basic level you can demonstrate the relative importance of the various parts of the message, thereby clarifying its meaning. In short, you will present the announcement in its most readily understandable form.

Oral communication, however, can be ineffective when the reader fails to present the material clearly. Too many flight attendants merely read words and consider themselves successful if they avoid stumbling over them. They forget that good communication between the flight attendant delivering the announcement and the passengers listening to the announcement occurs when the listener receives a meaningful impression of the information conveyed in the announcement.

Here are a few techniques:

Determine the parts of the announcement and its structure. On the most basic level, an announcement may be broken down into a beginning, middle, and end. The beginning is the introduction and customarily is used to gain attention. The middle, or body, contains most of the information. The end is generally used for summing up the most important points.

Analyze the punctuation to see what help it provides.

Note any words you do not fully understand or cannot pronounce. To deliver an announcement clearly, you must understand the meanings of words.

Correct pronunciation of words is as important as accurate understanding.

Whatever the purpose or nature of the announcement to be read, you must show interest in it if you are to communicate it effectively. Be interested in what you are saying. Even though you are reading from a prepared script and your audience knows it, they appreciate it when you sound as though you are not merely reading aloud.

Many airlines require flight attendant applicants to read a boarding card during the interview, to ensure that they have adequate verbal skills, so make it a habit to practice using correct speech in your daily life. If you have an obvious speech defect, or a shrill, weak, monotone or otherwise annoying voice, this will also distract from your presentation.

Work with a speech therapist to improve a voice problem or speech defect. All these things can interfere with your professional life in the workplace.

PRACTICE: READING ANNOUNCEMENTS ALOUD

Flight attendants also answer questions about the flight. Compose a two-minute description of a flight destination of your choice. Read through the copy, marking for emphasis, pronunciation, and so on. Read it aloud several times. When you are ready, tape your performance. Let your instructor make a critical evaluation of your performance.

Lesson 15: Answering questions on scenarios and stress management

Many of the major airlines use the scenario type of question typically at the second or third interview. This type of question gives you a situation that you may encounter while working as a flight attendant. It is a problem-solving question, requiring you to explain how you would handle various scenarios. Most of the scenario questions will put you in a situation on an airplane where a passenger has a problem.

EXERCISE: ANSWERING A SCENARIO INTERVIEW QUESTION

Here are a few of the more common scenario questions being asked at interviews. What would you say or do in each of these cases?

Question 1: A passenger in the economy class cabin says he noticed that the passengers in the first-class cabin were given pajamas and he would like one too.

Question 2: A woman changes her infant's diaper during the meal service and asks that you dispose of the dirty diaper for her.

Question 3: A man is trying to take a nap. He complains to you that he's having a hard time doing that because the baby next to him won't stop crying.

Lesson 16: Public speaking

Many people speak with an accent and many times, there are cultural differences in how we express ourselves. This, in itself, usually poses no problem. But the incorrect pronunciation of words or use of poor grammar will detract your professional image and lessen your chances of consideration for employment as a flight attendant.

No matter how impeccably a flight attendant candidate is dressed, it can make a recruiter's skin crawl to hear double negatives, slang words, cursing, mispronounced words or other such undignified grammatical errors.

This is the business world, and such indiscretions are unacceptable. Brush up on your speaking skills.

Knowing how to speak well and convincingly will help you get along better with other people.

The following pointers may help you:

Be prepared. Plan what you are going to say and practice it.

Take the time to warm up your voice on the way to the interview. Stretch and use your vocal cords before beginning the day of the interview. You will benefit with a clear and resonant voice.

Forget yourself. Forget that you are that you are too tall, or too short, too big or small, or that your facial features are less than perfect. Concentrate on the idea that you want to convey for this is far more important than what you are.

Relax. Before you say your piece, take a deep, but not audible, breath. Smile slightly as you look the audience over and establish eye contact. This will help you to feel at ease. It will also help make the audience feel that you are friendly.

Make some movement. If you feel that your knees are shaking, move a step or two. Putting one foot slightly in advance will keep you from swaying. Changing positions occasionally will help you be at ease.

Gestures should be spontaneous. They are a result of the desire to emphasize an idea, and therefore, must be made on the word you wish to emphasize.

ACTIVITY: PRACTICE INTERVIEW (Video-taped Session:)

Give answers to the following interview questions on scenarios and stress management. For each question, give yourself one minute to collect your thoughts before saying your answers aloud in front of a camera.

1. During your training sessions with a major international airline, your trainer gives you a hard time just because you are Asian, what will you do?

2. If you were to save only one person among these three passengers – a pregnant woman, a blind little boy, and an old male senior citizen – who would it be?

3. What major problem have you had to deal with recently?

4. What is the most difficult problem facing your country today and what should be done about it?

5. When do you feel down or depressed? How do you overcome the feeling?

Dos and Don'ts

- Although you are under pressure during a job interview, try to be relaxed, warm, open, and relatively energetic. Don't get flustered; speak clearly and calmly. Don't be too focused on how you are going to respond.

- If you don't fully understand a question, ask for it to be repeated. However, don't do this often or else the interviewer would think you have poor grasping power.

- Keep to the point and answer the question that has been asked. Don't get sidetracked and go off the point.

- Stay away from politics, religion, and sex. If the interviewer tries to lead you into any of these areas, politely avoid them.

- Be careful of traps. Some interviewers will lead job applicants along, making somewhat outrageous suggestions, to see if the applicant is an unprincipled "yes person." Do not be argumentative, but think carefully before you respond to questions that seem to be "off the wall."

- Be frank about your strengths and accomplishments, but take care not to come across as boastful.

- During group interviews, it's also crucial to show sensitivity to others' answers. Don't roll your eyes when you hear a mediocre answer.

- Do not be aggressive in asking about compensation.

- Never try to gain the sympathy of the person interviewing you by complaining about your problems.

Assessing Your Potential

SELF-ASSESSMENT CHECKLIST:

✓ Does my body language reflect the desirable qualities of a flight attendant?

✓ Am I able to correlate personal qualities to flight attendant duties?

✓ Am I able to listen carefully to questions and grasp ideas easily?

✓ Do I have excellent communication skills?

✓ Do I refrain from making derogatory remarks about my previous employer?

✓ Am I committed to becoming a flight attendant?

Enriching Your Skills

Before you appear for an interview, practice being interviewed. A friend or an instructor may be willing to assist you and to critique your performance. Remember that an interview is not acting, but it is a form of performance.

Video recording is the most effective form of interview practice that is used by many employment consulting firms, but if you own a camcorder, you can achieve the same results for a lot less money. To be most effective, you should have another individual acting as the interviewer. You should create an interview "set" and go through all the motions you would during an actual interview, from the introduction to the final handshake. The results of your videotaped interview can be very surprising. Very often, you will notice personal negative habits that you were perhaps never aware of. You should repeatedly tape the session until you are satisfied with your performance. Then, the actual interview should be a lot easier.

PRACTICE INTERVIEW QUESTIONS AND ANSWERS

❖ Questions on Personal History

1) **May I have your full name, please?**
What's your complete name?

My name is _____ .

2) **Tell me the meaning of your name.**

My first name is Seon Min. Seon Min are Chinese names. Seon, means to "lend" or give an aid to a person) and Min, the second name, means" to be mild". My grandfather gave me that name. I think that matches my personality because I like being kind to other people.

3) **Would you please tell me your age?**
How old are you?

I am 21 years old.

4) **When and where were you born?**

I was born on Mar. 18, 1986 in Busan.

5) **What is your permanent address?**

My permanent address is 123, OO Ree, OO Myon, OO Gun, Kyonggi-do.

I live in Bundang, which is a good place to live. The particular area where I live has fresh air and has a small number of people. In addition, it is suitable for exercise.

6) **Is your permanent address different from your present address?**

I still live in the same place.

No, I have only one address, and that's 123 O O Ree, OO Myon, OO Gun, Kyonggi-do.

7) **Where is your hometown?**

I live in Woo-dong, Haeundae-gu.

I was born in Daegu, but I spent my school days in Busan.

8) **What city are you from?**

I'm from Seoul.

Daegu is my hometown but I now live in Seoul. I finished my studies there.

9) **How long have you lived there?**

I lived there for about a couple of years.

I have lived there for 6 years. Before I settled there, I moved frequently.

10) **Tell me about your family.**

My family is perhaps the most supportive family in the world. My parents always remind us that a family should always stick together and support each other's decision and endeavor for as long as it is for our own good.

There are only three of us in the family: my father, mother and me. I used to wonder how it was like having a brother or a sister. But then I come to think of the fact that being the only child is really much better because I get to have things to myself anytime I want. I like it that way especially that my parents take really good care of me.

Ours is quite a big family. I've got four brothers and a sister. "The more, the merrier" is the family slogan. There's never a dull moment when all of us are together.

11) **Are your parents still alive?**

Yes, my parents are still alive.

No, both of them have passed away.

12) **How many brothers and sisters do you have?**

I have a brother and two sisters. I am the eldest of the brood.

13) **Are you single or married?**

I am still single at age twenty-two.

I am happily married.

I'm getting married soon.

14) **When are you going to get married?**
When are you planning to get married?

I still have a lot to explore so I'd probably get married when I'm twenty-five years old.

Honestly, I haven't thought of it yet. What's more important for me right now is to get a job that I really like.

15) **When did you get married?**

I got married last year.

I got married last spring.

16) **How long have you been married?**

I've been married for three years.

It was our 5th wedding anniversary a few days ago.

17) **How many sons and daughters do you have?**

We only have one child. We're planning our family.

18) **Do you support your family?**

Certainly. I am the breadwinner in the family. I'm the eldest son so I'm responsible to my parents.

_____

_____

_____

19) **What does your father do?**
What's your father's occupation?

My father has a meat shop. He sells insurance, too.

He is a government employee.

_____

_____

20) **Well, does your mother want you to get a job?**

Of course, she does. My mother hopes that before I'd get married I'd get a job in a company where I can use the skills and knowledge that I have learned in school.

_____

_____

_____

_____

21)   **Does your mother want you to quit your job when you marry?**

No, my mother leaves the decision to me. She says I am old enough to decide for myself.

_____

_____

22)   **Do you spend much time talking with your family?**

Oh yes. People say there's a generation gap in the world today, but I don't think there is one in our family. We all work on taking time to talk with each other. Especially at mealtimes, we all get together to eat and talk. Meals are very lively at our house.

_____

_____

_____

_____

_____

❖ Questions on Education and Professional Experience

1)   What is your major?

I majored in Tourism.

2)   Why did you choose to attend college abroad?

I have always wanted to travel to other places outside of my own country. So, when it was time to attend college, I asked my parents if they could afford to send me abroad for my studies. They agreed.

3)   Who were your favorite professors? Why?

My favorite professor was my instructor in engineering. He knew how to present his lessons well so that it would be easily understood by his students. He always monitored the progress of each student and made sure that no one was left behind.

4)   What was your favorite class? Why?

My favorite classes at the university were of course the ones handled by my favorite professor. I learned so many things from him.

5)   What was the class that you disliked?

I didn't like my science classes that much. It's too daunting for me.

6)   Tell me about the best and worst memories while you were in school.

My most memorable moment was in high school when I was awarded one of the top ten outstanding middle school students in the country. Imagine being picked out from millions of middle school students! It was a very big honor for our family. That's why it's my best memory in school... The worst memory I had was failing my Chemistry class.

7)   If given the chance and authority, what changes would you make at your college?

I would have wanted to have more exposure to the English language but the teachers in my school don't speak English all the time. They talk in their native tongue when they talk to their students outside of the classroom. So my proposal is for everybody – teachers and students – to speak or talk English all the time for as long as they are inside the school premises.

8)   How has your education prepared you for this career?

I took up Air and Tourism in college. If given the opportunity to work as a flight attendant, I would be able to put to good use what I have learned in college. My training in school included customer service, personality development, and communication, among other things. I am confident that with my training and educational background I would be able to build a career as a flight attendant.

9)   How can your education contribute to the work in this company?

I took up Air and Tourism in college. If given the opportunity to work as a flight attendant, I would be able to put to good use what I have learned in college. My training in school included customer service, personality development, and communication, among other things. I am confident that with my training and educational background I would be able to contribute a lot to this airline.

10)   Do you have any plans for further education?

Apart from the flight attendants training or anything related to this career, I don't have any immediate plans of studying further. I'd like to concentrate on flying.

11)   Tell me about your experience.

TIP: Your answer should focus only on experiences that apply to the flight attendant position, such as customer service and safety. Cite at least one achievement from either your educational and professional experiences.

I have eight years of customer service experience. I started as a customer care representative who handled complaints and queries from customers of the company. After four years, I moved up to a supervising position where I had six customer care representatives in my team. After two more years I was already the chief of our division.

❖ Questions on Physical Condition

1) **What's your blood type?**

It's type O.

---

2) **What is your height?**

It's 172 centimeters.

How tall are you?
I'm 172 centimeters tall.

---

4) **What is your weight?**

It's 64 kilograms.

How much do you weigh?
I weigh 64 kilograms.

---

5) **What is your eyesight?**

My left eyesight is 1.5 and my right eyesight is 1.2

How is your vision?

I have a pretty good vision. It's both 1.5.

_____

_____

6) How's your health condition?

Are you in good health?

I think I am very healthy. I am seldom sick.

I had poor health when I was young but my health improved during middle school
days. I've been in good health since.

_____

_____

_____

7) Have you had a physical check up?

a. Yes, I have. I am in good health.

b. No, I haven't been to the doctor yet.

_____

_____

8) What do you do to keep in good physical condition?

What do you keep in mind for your health?

a. I enjoy sports and I try to keep good hours. I do a lot of exercise and eat a
balanced diet.

b. I try to eat properly, take moderate exercises and get a good sleep.

_____

_____

_____

9) **Do you have any visible scars?**

I have none. Fortunately, I haven't had any operation to leave visible scars on my body.

_____

_____

_____

10) **The job of a flight attendant requires you to stand for hours. Can you do that?**

Yes, I can stand for hours. I'm very healthy. I exercise more than three times a week, so I'm very well disciplined physically.

_____

_____

_____

_____

❖ Questions on Communication

1) **How many foreign languages do you speak?**
What languages can you speak?

I speak English and Japanese fluently.

I can speak English and Japanese. I took language lessons at school.

I understand a little English, but I can't speak it very well.

_____

_____

_____

2) **How long have you studied Japanese?**

I studied Japanese for 10 years from my high school days.

I learned Japanese during my school days, but I didn't have a chance to practice conversation.

_____

_____

_____

_____

3) **Can you speak any language besides English?**

I can speak German and Japanese aside from English.

_____

_____

_____

4) **Where do you study English?**
Where have you studied English?

I study English at a private institute.

I have studied English on campus and at a private institute.

_____

_____

5) **Is your English getting better now?**

Yes, it is. I have been studying English so hard.

_____

_____

_____

6) **Do you have many opportunities to practice your English with foreigners?**

No, not many. I only get to practice English with foreigners occasionally.

I get to speak English with foreigners only once in a blue moon.

_____

_____

_____

7) **Are you nervous about your English?**

Yes I am. I'm afraid I might make mistakes.

No, I'm not. I see no reason why I should be.

_____

_____

_____

8) **Are you afraid of making mistakes when you speak English?**

No, not at all. I speak fluent English.

I'm a bit afraid. Sometimes I feel shy. However, I know that if one wants to speak English well, he has to speak it with confidence. It won't be long and I'll be speaking English with ease.

_____

_____

_____

Questions on Career Potential
(Knowledge and Interest in the Profession)

1) What brings you here?

I want to be a flight attendant of _____ Airlines.

2) When did you decide on this career?

I decided to become a flight attendant after learning from an acquaintance how great this job is. You get to meet a lot of people and make new friends in the process. Besides, I wanted to do something different after working as a customer care representative at a big department store in our city for eight years.

_____

_____

_____

Tell me why you are applying for this job.

I lost interest in working on never-ending projects. After ten years, I thought I've had enough. I'd try something that is more finite like being a flight attendant. I find this job more appealing.

3) What made you interested in applying for a position as a flight attendant?

So you would like to become a flight attendant. What made you decide on this type of occupation?

I wanted a job working with people, not at a desk doing paper work. I enjoy meeting different kinds of people and travelling, so being a flight attendant is right up my alley.

_____

_____

_____

4) How did you hear about the job?

The employment consultant of my college recommended me to this company.

A friend of mine who is working here told me that your company had an opening.

_____

_____

_____

5) Can you tell us anything you know about our company?

Singapore Airlines ranks 6th in the world for international passengers carried and ranks 17th in Fortune's World's Most Admired Companies in 2007. Your airline has a presence in the airline markets of Southeast Asia, East Asia, South Asia and the competitive "kangaroo route" between Europe and Oceania. Singapore Airlines operates two of the world's longest non-stop commercial flights from Singapore to Newark, New Jersey and Los Angeles, California.

6) What are the changes of Qatar Airlines over the past year / in a year?

TIP: You should do some research about the company. Know some basic information about them, including the latest developments in their airline, in particular, and the airline industry, in general.

7) What do you know of the country-base of the airlines?

TIP: Before you go for an airline interview, you should have a basic knowledge of where they fly and find out their major hubs.

8) What are the qualifications needed to become a flight attendant?

What are the qualifications of a cabin crew?

> 3. *A flight attendant, above all, has to be a people person with good language and communication skills. He / She has to be highly enthusiastic, flexible, dependable and trustworthy. A flight attendant must also be diligent and works independently without supervision. In addition, he / she must have stamina and good health.*

9) Do you possess the skills necessary to perform in an effortless manner as a flight attendant?

Do you believe that you are qualified to become a flight attendant? If so, what makes you think that?

> *I have a naturally friendly, positive communication style. I am healthy, kind and patient. I could very well use these traits if I become a flight attendant for your airline.*

> *Not only do I have a healthy body and good manners, but I am also diligent, honest and warm-hearted. I am interested in foreign countries and speak a couple of foreign languages as well. I am equipped with just about everything that is required of a flight attendant.*

---

10) What do you think the flight attendant's primary responsibility is as a crew member?

> *Providing exemplary customer service to passengers desiring to travel by performing or assisting in the performance of all safety, passenger service, and cabin preparation duties.*

11) Why should I hire you?

What can you contribute that separates you from the other candidates?

> *I have a lot to offer your airlines. I am a people person with a strong professional background in customer care and management. I am a team player. I am highly enthusiastic and flexible. I am willing to relocate to any base.*

12) **Do you like routine schedules or do you prefer different work hours for you job?**

I get bored with routine schedules. I'd like some unpredictability when it comes to my work.

I think that changes are interesting. I don't mind any work schedule. I am flexible.

_____

_____

_____

_____

13) **How familiar are you with the community that we are located in?**

Honestly speaking, I have only been here a week but the friend that I am staying with temporarily has been very gracious to show me around. I am impressed with what I have seen so far. It is quite different from where I lived.

14) **Are you a goal-oriented person?**

Yes, I am a goal-oriented person. In fact, becoming a flight attendant is a goal that I have set for myself since high school. I just wasn't able to apply sooner because I had to give in to my parents' wishes. They wanted me to help in the family business for a couple of years before I could pursue a career in the skies.

15) **What goals do you have in your career?**

I want to fly international in a couple of years.

How do you plan to achieve these goals?

4. *I am going to study really hard during training and be one of the best in the class. Be prepared to be away from home quite a lot and be prepared to have fun working on weekends or holidays.*

What are your short-term goals?

5. *Flying international is on top of all my short-term goals. I'd also like to go on a vacation at the Bahamas with my family.*

What do you see yourself doing five years from now?

6. *If I get this job, I know I would still be with this airline. By that time, I shall*

have been flying international, doing a great job and above all, enjoying it a lot.

What is your long-range objective?

7. *My long-range objective is to build my dream house in a plush neighborhood and send my kids to the best schools.*

How much training do you think you'll need to become a productive employee?

8. *A month or two would be enough. I learn fast.*

How do you personally define success? / What is your definition of success?

9. *Success is achieving your targets on time and being a role model in the eyes of another person.*

Describe a situation in which you were successful.

10. *I was taken as a new account executive at an advertising agency straight from college. I didn't have any actual work experience except my 6-month internship before graduation so I was really jittery at the start of my job. I was given a quota of five new clients a month. The first month was very frustrating; I got only one account! The second month wasn't any better than the first. I cried and begged my supervisor for another chance. Then I read marketing books during my free time and learned some tactics on how to corner the best accounts and voila! I made it! Five accounts on my third month. From then on I was exceeding my quota on average.*

Have you ever suffered setbacks or failures?
Tell me an experience when you felt discouraged or frustrated.

11. *Oh, yes. I was forced to quit college because of financial constraints. My father lost his job unexpectedly and the family didn't have any savings for me to continue with my studies. I stopped studying for six months.*

What accomplishments have given you the most satisfaction in your life?

12. *The single accomplishment that has given me the most satisfaction to date is working to pay for my studies. I worked my way through college after my father suddenly lost his job and couldn't financially support my studies anymore. That experience taught me that if you really wanted something so badly, you would do anything to get it.*

How would you describe your ideal job?

13. My ideal job is a job that allows me to be with people and do something for them.

About travel:

Which country / countries have you ever been to?

I've been to the Philippines to study.

Did you ever feel any difficulties or did you have any culture shock?

I did have some culture shock when I traveled to the Philippines. It's quite different from my native country in a number of ways.

What have you learned in your travels abroad?

I learned how to adapt to foreign cultures and accept the ways of other peoples.

Aside from studying, what were the things you did or experienced?

I explored the many attractive tourist spots in the Philippines and visited a lot of heritage sites of the country. I also made friends with a lot of people there.

If you were a flight attendant, what do you expect to be the most difficult task while on board or flying?

14. According to a flight attendant I talked to on my flight here, passengers that have been drinking or acting irrationally are the most difficult to handle. So I guess I'd expect the same thing if I were a flight attendant.

How can you overcome the homesickness while staying abroad or away from your home country?

15. I'll communicate regularly with my family and friends back home. With our technology today, that would not be a problem.

Are you willing to travel? How much?

16. I am very willing to travel. That's the nature of a flight attendant's job. I am available for you at any time and any location.

Do you have any location preferences?

17. I don't have any preferences. I can go anywhere.

Are you willing to relocate in the future?

18. Yes, I am at your disposal.

Are you prepared to move anywhere at any time to further your career?

19. I am absolutely prepared to go anywhere if it's good for my career.

_____

_____

_____

_____

What qualities do you feel a successful manager should have?

20. A successful manager should be someone whose leadership style takes into account the rights and interests of his subordinates.

What kind of salary are you looking for?

21. I would like a salary that is commensurate to my performance and abilities and to the hazards of the job.

What is your favorite cocktail? Explain how it is done.

22. My favorite drink is Atlas. It's so easy to make. Just mix two parts Vodka, preferably Senator's Club, and one part Blue Curacao, and a splash of orange juice and fill with cranberry juice. Mix all of these ingredients in a shaker with ice. Strain and then serve!

Are you interested in domestic or international flights?

23. My goal would be to fly on international flights, but I realize I must begin with domestic flights.

_____

_____

_____

_____

Your work experience to date has been outside of the airline industry. What are your feelings regarding the lifestyle changes a flight attendant career will bring?

> 24. *That is true. I have never worked for an airline before but I have always dreamed of becoming a flight attendant. I ask every flight attendant I would meet along the way what his or her life is like and I have learned all sorts of things about the life of a flight attendant, including the bad ones. But I still want to work in the skies and I am willing to do what it takes to be a good flight attendant.*

What are the strengths and weaknesses of a cabin attendant's life? How will you get over (overcome) the weak points?

What are the rewards and stresses of a flight attendant's life? How do you deal with the stresses?

> 25. *The good thing about the life of a cabin crew attendant is traveling to other places especially abroad. That's what excites me about this job. Other people pay to go places but a flight attendant gets paid to see other places. However, the work can be strenuous and difficult, especially when you have stressful passengers on board. But that can be worked out. If given the opportunity to be part of this airlines, I won't let stressful passengers get on my nerves. I am a very patient and calm person so I think I wouldn't have a problem dealing with difficult passengers.*

Are you willing to work long hours?

Sometimes a flight attendant must work long hours. Would this be a problem for you?

> 26. *Not at all. I don't mind working long hours. I got used to that in my previous work.*

_____

_____

Are you willing to start at the very bottom of the ladder?

   27. Yes, I am. Everybody has to start somewhere.

❖ Questions on Personality and Behavior

What kind of personality do you think you have?

What can you say about your character?
Describe your personality to me.

      A. *I like to think of myself as a balanced person. I enjoy the company of other people, but sometimes I like to be alone to work or just think. I focus hard on the things that are necessary, but when I have some time off, I like to sit back and relax.*

      B. *I am a good listener and a cooperative person.*

---

2. Do you think you have a good personality?

      A. *I believe so. My friends say I have a great personality.*

3. Would you describe yourself as outgoing or reserved?
(Do you think you are outward looking or inward looking?)

A. I can be both. It depends on the situation and who I am with.

B. Well, most of the time I like being around people and doing things with people, so I guess I'm more of the outgoing type. That's why I was very active in my university club.

C. Well, I'm not very outgoing, but I can deal with people if the occasion calls for it.

_____

_____

_____

_____

4. Are you more of a follower or a leader?

A. I'd say I'm good at being a follower but if there is a need for me to be at the forefront of things, I don't balk at the responsibility.

B. They say a good leader is a good follower. And I believe that. I am ready to follow a leader who has the best ideas and knows what's best for the team. On the other hand, I am ready to take charge if it's necessary.

C. I don't agree with someone else's opinion right away but if I see his point and it's good, then I would no longer have any second thoughts about cooperating.

D. I don't try to get in front of people and lead them, particularly. I would rather cooperate with everybody else, and get the job done by working together.

_____

_____

_____

_____

_____

_____

5. What would you say are some of your strong points?
(What are your good qualities?)

A. *I have two good points about myself. First, I am optimistic and always try to look on the bright side of things. Second, I always try to do my best. I can easily adapt myself to any circumstances.*

B. *I consider frankness as one of my good qualities. I speak my mind even if others do not share my point of view. Who knows they might find my idea better than the rest? They say it only takes one man with courage to make a majority.*

C. *I am a straightforward type of person. No pretenses. I say things as they are, even if I would get hurt by doing so. However, I am quick to admit a mistake and learn from it.*

D. *My best quality is my humor. I feel happy when people enjoy listening to my stories.*

E. *I am considerate of other people, especially their shortcomings. I believe a failure will bring another chance. That's my motto. That's why I try not to be biased in life but to find a lot of possibilities in it.*

_____

_____

_____

_____

_____

6. What is your greatest strength?

A. *My greatest strength is on interpersonal skills. I can usually win people over to my side to see my point of view. In addition, I think I have good judgment about people.*

7. What is your hobby?

A. *I love collecting angel figurines. Since I was a little girl, I have always been fascinated with drawings or any representation of angels.*

8. Tell me about your strengths and weaknesses.

A. *I'm strong in positive thinking and concentration. My down side is that I care too much about little stuffs but I am trying to change that now.*

B. *I like developing new things and ideas but I have difficulty expressing them because I am a poor talker. But I have been studying how to speak in public.*

C. *I am quick in learning languages, but my computer experience is somewhat limited. However, I recently took a weeklong training program on using the MAC and I'm looking forward to building on the skills I learned.*

_____

_____

9. What is your weakness?

A. My weakness is making decisions hastily. I am afraid I'm quite impatient.

B. My weakness is food. I love gourmet food.

C. I lack a sense of adventure. Whenever I have some free time, I prefer to stay at home and do things by myself instead of going out with friends.

_____

_____

_____

_____

10. Tell me what your worst habit is.

A. My worst habit is spending a lot of time on the phone. I know people who are really good at having short conversations on the phone, but I can't do that. If a friend is on the phone, I want to talk for an hour.

_____

_____

_____

_____

_____

11. Do you usually mix with others?

Are you sociable?

A.   *I have a very sociable personality. I enjoy being with other people.*

_____

_____

_____

_____

12. Do you like meeting new people?

A.   *That's my preoccupation. I love to make new friends.*

_____

_____

_____

_____

13. Do you think you give a good impression to others?

A.   *I think so. People who know me are impressed with my punctuality and positive attitude to things.*

_____

_____

14. Do you think you are ambitious?

A. *I am. I believe every person should have an ambition or else he wouldn't have any direction at all. If a man had no ambition, what then is he living for?*

15. Do you think you have responsibility?

A. *I am a responsible person. I take responsibility for every action that I do and every word that I say. I don't give up until a task is done and I don't blame anybody if I don't finish it on time.*

B. *People tell me I have a strong sense of responsibility because I go beyond what is expected of me to get things done.*

16. How do your friends describe you?

A. *Aside from my being sincere and diligent, those who know me say I'm also a faithful person.*

B. *People say I am optimistic, cheerful, and hardworking.*

_____

_____

_____

_____

17. Would you rather work with information or with people?

A. *People, of course. There is more diversity and dynamism in people than in information.*

18. What makes you angry?

A. *I am not easily angered; however, I particularly dislike overbearing, over-aggressive egotistical behavior.*

_____

_____

_____

_____

19. Which one makes you angry the most at work, e.g. (breaking

engagements, lie, impolite people)

A. *I am not easily angered, especially at work. I have a lot of patience. I keep my cool most of the time. Besides, if there is anything that I don't like, I don't show my disappointment or my anger.*

20. What inspires you?

A. *When I see people being passionate about what they do and really care about. I like seeing them get into it.*

_____

_____

_____

_____

21. What is your principle in life?

A. *Never surrender. That's how I look at the challenges in life. I won't give up no matter how difficult the situation.*

22. What motivates you?

A. *Hunger for the best. That is what motivates me in everything I do.*

23. Is money important to you?

A. *Yes, money is important to me but not as important as relationships. I believe it when they say good relationships are at the heart of happiness. Money doesn't buy happiness.*

24. How much money do you need to make to be happy?

A. *I don't need to make so much money to be happy. I only need enough to spend for my own needs and the needs of my family and save for recreation and our future.*

25. Who do you admire the most?

A. *I admire _____ because of his accomplishments in life. He inspires me.*

26. What is the one lesson you learned as a child that still affects your life today?

A. *I learned that a lie does not solve a problem in the past; it even creates another problem in the future. I once told a lie to save myself from my mother's spanking. I stood by my fabricated story and told one more lie after another until such time that I could no longer keep track of what lies I told to every particular person without being found out that I was lying. My credibility crumbled.*

27. Which color do you like the most?

A. *I like blue. It's a royal color. It has a pacifying effect on me.*

28. Tell me, who is the personality that best represents you as a person? Explain your choice.

A. *I choose Queen Victoria of England. I think I am like her in a smaller*

way. Queen Victoria ascended to the throne at a very young age but she never married. Instead, she dedicated her life to governing England to bring the kingdom to greatness. She sacrificed herself for the greater glory. I am like that, too. I am ready to make sacrifices for the greater good.

29. If you became a leader of your country tomorrow, what would be the first thing you would do?

A. *I would reset the standards of performance of the government workers. By doing this, I would be able to weed out the misfits in government service.*

30. If you had the power to do anything you wished to improve the status of women in your country, what would you do?

A. *I would ask Congress to review all the laws that have anything to do with women and ask them to amend those that are unfavorable to women.*

31. What is the most precious gift you have given to someone?

A. *For me, quality time can not be quantified monetarily. Considering the busy person that I am, I seldom find time to party or loiter around. So I think the most precious gift I have given to someone is my time. I took a week off from work to be some sort of a tour guide to my sister who that time was on vacation after graduating from high school. It was what I called my graduation gift to her.*

32. If you could choose what time

period to be born and what sex to be, what would you choose and why?

A. *If I had the choice, I would rather be born a female during the time of Queen Victoria of England. In my readings, the Victorian Age was one of the best times of the history of England. During Queen Victoria's reign, England enjoyed economic prosperity and intellectual development to the hilt. Her rule was an affirmation that women were just as good as the men, perhaps even better.*

33. What is the biggest challenge in your life?

A. *The biggest challenge of my life is overcoming my grief over the death of a loved one. Losing him was the most difficult part of my life. It is a big challenge to wake up each day and not think of him and cry inside.*

34. If I were to ask one of your professors (or a boss) to describe you, what would he or she say?

A. *I know they'd say that I am a punctual and hardworking person with a positive attitude towards things. If there is a task in front of me, I will not stop until I have finished it.*

35. What personal characteristics are necessary for success in your chosen field?

A. *What do you think it takes to be successful in this career?*

B. *I believe that honesty and hard work are necessary to succeed in this field.*

C. *Punctual, well-organized, and quick learner are words that would best*

describe me. I believe these are personal characteristics that would make me succeed as a flight attendant.

_____

_____

_____

_____

_____

_____

❖ Questions on Teamwork and Group Participation

1) Do you believe in teamwork?

I do. A team can benefit from the combined input and ideas of all its members. The amount of work for each person can be much lesser because the team's workload can be divided among the members.

_____

_____

_____

_____

_____

_____

2) What do you think are the advantages and disadvantages to the team-based approach?
Talk about the negative / positive points of teamwork.

3)   *The pace of work is slower in the team-based approach. Teams face problems such as not agreeing on important issues which results in tardy decisions and actions. Team projects are sometimes of lower quality than the individual projects because the final result shows the compromise in style among all the members. However, if the final result isn't perfect, the blame is shared among the team, which isn't as bad as taking all the blame on oneself.*

_____

_____

_____

_____

_____

4) What do you enjoy most about working as part of a team?

5)   *I like listening to the exchange of ideas and seeing the cooperation of the members. The best part of a team activity is the feeling you get after completing the task that was assigned to the team.*

_____

_____

_____

_____

_____

6) Are you a team player?

7)   *Yes, I am. I get along well with a group. In fact, I like it even better than doing things by myself.*

8) When you work with a team, what is important?

9)   *It's important to participate and give inputs to the team in order to accomplish the task at hand.*

10) Do you prefer working with others or by yourself?

11)   *I like working with others. The more the merrier.*

_____

_____

_____

_____

12) What's the most difficult about working with colleagues?

13)   *For me, the most difficult part about working with colleagues is adjusting to a person with an attitude. It's really a challenge to get along with somebody like that.*

14) Tell us about your experience working on a team.

15)   *Working with a team is great. There's just all sorts of ideas and you get to know more about the people you are working with because of the time that you spend together as*

a team. However, I have observed that when the team is under pressure, the individual attitudes get in the way and the team spirit is lost.

16) Describe your ideal co-worker.

17)   For me, an ideal co-worker would be someone who is your partner in every step of the way. It would be somebody who considers other people's interests and rights as important as his.

18) How do you contribute to make the team that you join even better?

How can you make a good teamwork?

19)   I would help the team to lessen the load by breaking down tasks into manageable ones.
20)   I will not stop until I shall have finished the tasks given to me. I will provide leadership and direction, if necessary, and assistance to other members of the team who would have a hard time completing their own assignments.

21) Do you enjoy doing independent research?

It's fun doing some research especially if it is about airlines and flight attendants.

22) If your first project were to develop an advertising campaign of a new cosmetic product, please explain what your plan would be.

23)   Since the target markets of cosmetic products are women, I would concentrate on women's magazines and TV ads on time slots when a lot of women are watching TV. I would try to find out the advantages of the new product over all the other similar products in the market. My ads would emphasize my product's advantages.

24)   I would first learn about the product and figure out which age groups would likely purchase the product. Then based on the buying habits and likes and dislikes of these age groups, I would design appealing magazine, TV, radio, newspaper, billboard advertisements and where they need to be concentrated in order to get the highest

return on the advertising investment.

_____

_____

_____

_____

_____

_____

_____

❖ Questions on In-Flight Scenarios and Stress Management

1) How well do you take stress? How do you handle stress?

2) *I take stress positively. For me, some stress is productive. It makes me a better person. So when I am stressed out, I meditate. I do yoga exercises and take a lot of rest.*

3) *I believe that a little stress once in a while is better than no stress at all. When I am so worn out, I go to bed early and sleep. If it doesn't work, I go find a quiet place and cry out loud. After that, I feel good.*

_____

_____

_____

_____

4) Do you have a lot of patience with other people? A flight attendant must deal with all kinds of people and remain courteous.

5) *I have a lot of patience. I don't easily get angry or frustrated. I guess it comes from six years of experience in customer service.*

_____

_____

_____

_____

_____

6) Sometimes a flight attendant must work long hours and have an unusual schedule, would this be a problem for you?

7) *No, not at all. I like changes, not routine. And I don't mind working long hours. I got used to doing that in my previous job as a customer service representative.*

_____

_____

_____

_____

8) Do you handle conflict well?

9) *I can handle conflict well. Conflict at work is inevitable but I believe that to some*

degree it's good because it shows the dynamism among the employees. It eliminates monotony in the workplace, too.

10) How do you handle conflict?

11)   *I keep the communication lines open. I honestly express my feelings in a way that also takes into consideration the feelings and rights of other people. I avoid being aggressive. Most importantly, I try being conciliatory to avoid the stress of a conflict.*

12) Have you ever had a conflict with a boss or professor? How did you resolve it?

13)   *Oh yes, I did have a conflict with my science professor. He gave me a poor grade. I thought I deserved a higher grade because I was studying hard in his class. I pointed out to him that I was getting good scores in the tests and making good projects. At first, he wouldn't hear of it. He just told me I could have done better if I wanted a higher grade. But I kept pursuing the issue. Later on he acknowledged his mistake. He found out he had interchanged my grade with that of another student.*

14) Do you handle pressure well?

I handle pressure positively. I think working under pressure sometimes is productive. As far as I am concerned, it makes me perform better.

15) What would you do if a passenger on the flight was being rude to you?

16)   *In customer service the customer is always right so I would do everything in my capacity to calm him down and help him enjoy the flight.*

_____

_____

_____

_____

17) How do you handle sexual harassment like a passenger touching your hips or butt?

18)   *I will tell the passenger calmly that what he did was improper and that I wouldn't tolerate it if he did it again.*

19) What would you do if you had an unhappy passenger on the plane?

20)   *I'm going to talk to the passenger calmly and ask him what his problem is then try to solve it to his satisfaction. If the solution to his problem is against company or airline regulations, then I would explain him why his request couldn't be accommodated.*

_____

_____

_____

_____

21) How would you handle an irate passenger?

I would calmly ask him what made him angry and listen to what he has to say. Then I would acknowledge his problem and explain to him what I could do to make him feel better.

22) How would you conduct yourself in case of an emergency during flight?

23)   *I'll do my best to calm down then remind myself of emergency procedures I've learned and follow the supervisor's instructions.*

_____

_____

_____

_____

_____

24) A passenger in the economy class says he noticed that the passengers in the first-class cabin were given pajamas and he would like one, too.

25) *I should explain to the passenger that one of the amenities offered to first class passengers is a complimentary pajama and that in reality they are paying for the pajama because of the increased ticket price. I would also say that I would do my best to accommodate him by checking if there are extra pajamas.*

_____

_____

_____

_____

_____

26) A woman changes her infant's diapers during the meal service and asks that you dispose of the dirty diaper for her.

27) *I should advise the passenger that I would be happy to dispose of the diaper once I'm finished with the meal service. I could also recommend that the passenger dispose of the diaper herself in the lavatory. In either case, I should recommend that she put the diaper inside an airsickness bag prior to disposal.*

_____

_____

_____

_____

_____

_____

_____

28) You spilled tomato juice or hot coffee on a passenger due to sudden turbulence. What would you say to the passenger?

29)   *The first thing I would do is to apologize for my mistake then I would ask him the best way to compensate. I would try to follow his/her suggestion within the limits of the company's regulations.*

_____

_____

_____

_____

_____

30) A man is trying to take a nap. He complains to you that he's having a hard time doing that because the baby next

to him won't stop crying.

31)   *If the flight is not completely full, I should ask the passenger if he would like to change seats and relocate to a quieter location. If he is not willing to move, I could also ask the person with the baby if she would mind moving.*

_____

_____

_____

_____

_____

_____

_____

Arab Emirate & Qatar Discussion

1) Where do you want to travel with your parents?

My parents and I have always wanted to go to Europe. Once I become a flight attendant, I'm going to bring my parents to the fascinating sights in that part of the world.

2) If your friend feels down, how can you cheer her / him up?

First, I'll ask him to share his problem with me and I'll lend him an ear. Then I'll offer some options that I would take if I were in his shoes. And then I would take him out to a funny movie.

3) If you were to go out with a handicapped person, where would you bring him or her? Why?

I'd bring him or her to a park, mall or any place that has amenities for people with disabilities so that he or she will not be having a hard time moving about. I wouldn't want to bring him or her on a nature trip like hiking or mountain climbing because it would be so laborious on his part.

4) What is your most embarrassing moment?

My most embarrassing moment was when I was mistaken for a gay. I couldn't believe anyone would think I'm gay because of my haircut.

5) What kind / type of person would you like to work and what kind / type of person wouldn't you like to work with?

I wouldn't want to work with a person who would just love to watch you do the dirty work then take credit for everything especially when the end product is appreciated by other people. I want to work with a person who shares his ideas with the group and cooperates.

6) What kind of gift do you want to give as a birthday present for a handicapped / disabled person?

I would give him a gift that he could use, something that would help him deal with his handicap.

7)   What (do you think) are the challenges of living abroad? How would you deal with them?

     Suppose you live in Doha, what would be the difficulties and how could you overcome such?

Living abroad isn't easy. You have to deal with the loneliness being away from your family and friends. And when something happens to you or you get sick, you have no one to turn to unless you have made another circle of friends in the foreign land. Aside from that, you also experience what they call culture shock. There's also the language barrier. So if I were to live abroad, I need to build bridges of friendship to deal with the loneliness. I will establish another network of friends who would be able to help me adjust to their culture and teach me the nuances of their language. I will also communicate regularly with my family and friends back home. With all the modern technologies that are available to us nowadays, communication would not be much of a problem.

8)   Give me five factors, which can affect a flight attendants promotion.

I believe the ability to cooperate in group endeavors, impeccable service to passengers, excellent communication skills, good work ethics, and seniority have a great bearing on the promotion of a flight attendant.

9)   Talk about culture shock with a partner. (For pair interview)

Culture shock happens when you are immersed in a new environment that is very dissimilar to where you are from or what you have been used to. But I don't think culture shock is really that bad. You just have to adjust to your new environment – adjust to the new people around you and adopt their ways and how they do things in their homeland. I believe it is not wise to impose your own ways on these people. It's better to accept them as they are so that you wouldn't be as shocked.

10)   Introduce the hobby of your partner.

My partner is into mixed martial arts. Kind of a grueling type of hobby, if you ask me, but it's a great sports activity that really shows what kind of stuff you are made of.

11)   Talk about your favorite dish / menu, the ingredients, the process of cooking, etc.

My favorite dish is a one-dish meal pasta salad. It's very easy to do. Just slice and drain a can of hearts of palm. Break a small head of broccoli into small flowerets. Chop a red bell pepper coarsely. Slice three stalks of celery and six green onions. Cook eight ounces of pasta of your choice al dente. Then add all other ingredients

including 6 ½ ounces of marinated artichoke hearts. If you don't like artichoke hearts then you can substitute it with avocado. If desired, add a little lemon juice or rice vinegar. It's best eaten if it's chilled.

12) Why should flight attendants be independent?

Flight attendants should be independent because they are the ones who take care of the passengers during a flight. They provide assistance during an emergency and administer first aid to ill or incapacitated passengers. A person who is not independent can't do those things.

13) Talk about the disadvantages / advantages of using a cell phone.

The cell phone connects you to anyone at anytime from any part of the world where there is a signal. However, you can get into trouble if someone else uses your cell phone for something illegal.

14) Why do you think time management is important?

Time management is important. The better you organize your time, the more tasks you get done whether it is on the job or simply doing housework.

15) Why are company regulations important?

Company regulations are important because they regulate how we do our work and help us get along with our co-workers. Company regulations also set standards to job performance.

16) What is the biggest mistake in your life?

(TIP: This question has to be answered based on experience. For your answer to have some weight, narrate the experience where you made the biggest mistake of your life.)

The biggest mistake in my life was trusting someone right away without getting to know him thoroughly first. That mistake cost my job…

17) Tell me three advantages / three disadvantages of living in a multicultural country.

If you live in a multicultural country, you are exposed to different ways of life – their culture, beliefs, food, language and habits. You have variety. With this exposure, you learn to tolerate the differences with your own culture and it makes you more understanding of not just their cultures but also your own. I think that makes you a better person because you have less prejudice against other citizens of the world… One disadvantage I can think of about living in a multicultural country is the possibility of getting in conflict with an extremist or racist who is hostile to the idea of having other nationalities in their country.

18) Is it a sin to tell a lie?

If I take it from a Christian point of view, lying is a sin no matter what, even if the intention is good. With morality as the yardstick, I believe some lies are necessary and they are not wrong especially if they are done out of empathy and compassion.

19)   Tell me about your most preferred job except being a flight attendant.

I'd like to be a hotel concierge. I like the challenge of catering to the wishes and requests of hotel guests.

20)   There are eight people in an island, five people are physically well / sound, and 3 need rescue / care. Among the three injured, one is an old citizen suffering from a cardiac arrest, one is a pregnant woman and the last is a 5 year-old disabled girl, you can only save one. Who would you choose and why?

I choose to save the pregnant woman because she has another life inside her. If I would save her, I'd be saving two lives.

21)   What was the most unforgettable experience in your part-time job, if any?

The most unforgettable experience I've had while working as a part-time TV newscaster was stuttering towards the end of the newscast. I was so consumed by sheer nervousness that I simply could not remember my own name! Unimaginable but true.

22)   Talk about the most impressive tourism points with a partner.

23)   In Korean culture, what are five things that may cause misunderstanding?

24)   What are three things you think can make Korea prosper even further?

SAMPLE QUESTIONS FOR DISCUSSION

1)   There is a passenger suffering from airsickness, how can you deal / handle the situation?

I will advise the passenger to close her eyes and relax or bring her an MP3 player to keep him or her preoccupied. And if she's hungry, I'll give her some raw vegetables, pretzels or plain potato chips, whichever she likes.

2) Which nationality do you prefer to live with as a flat mate and which nationality do you prefer not to live with as a flat mate? Give five reasons each.

3) If you were to go to a planet, what ten items would you bring and why?

If I were to go to a planet, I would bring the basics like water, food, vitamins, over the counter medicines, toothpaste, toothbrush, sleeping bag, tent, clothes and moisturizer.

4) What kind of gift do you want to give as a birthday present for a disabled person?

5) Choose five celebrities / public figures you would want to invite to your dinner party.

Granting that I have the power and influence to gather these people, I would invite any of the Nobel Prize for Peace winners, the president or monarch of any of the Arab countries, an economic minister from any European Union country, Charice Pempengco of the Philippines and Pope Benedict XVI. It would be the greatest opportunity to be around these personalities from whom we could learn so much about propagating world peace and prosperity.

6) If you were to rate yourself on a scale of one to ten, how many points will you give to yourself and why?

I would give myself ten points. I believe I have all it takes to be a good flight attendant.

7) If only one person can have a cardiac / heart operation, which of the following people do you want to give the chance to: a ten year old genius girl, a brain surgeon who has 90 % probability success, a thirty year old 3-month pregnant woman.

Operating on the pregnant woman would be risky because a heart operation is a major surgery and should not be done on pregnant women. Between the ten year old genius and the brain surgeon, I'd give the chance to the brain surgeon because of the fact that if he would be operated on, the operation would probably be 90 percent successful. Compared to the ten year old genius girl, the brain surgeon will have more contributions to society if his heart becomes well and he goes back to practicing his profession.

8) Choose a personal gift for your interviewer. (You may ask 3 questions to your interviewer)

(TIP: You may ask the interviewer the following questions. What particular product of Korea do you like? Whatever it is and if you can afford it, then that would be your gift for the interviewer. If he doesn't like anything Korean, then find out if he travels a lot. If he does then give him an item that would be useful or practical while traveling.)

9) If you were an interviewer, which applicants would you choose? There are 100 applicants and all of them are qualified but you have to choose 10 of them. What are your standards?

I'd choose the ten most qualified applicants based on their knowledge of all safety, passenger service and cabin preparation duties. I'd also choose the top ten in terms of personality, communication skills, work attitude, flexibility, customer service, stress and emergency management.

10) Your colleague is suffering from a bad rumor, what would you do to help her / him?

I would tell my colleague to be unaffected and just let the rumor pass. What is heard through the grapevine will eventually die out anyway. Unless the rumor affects his job or studies directly, I would advise him that he is not obliged to clear his name because he is not answerable to anyone but himself. I would also assure him that the rumor is not affecting my relationship with him.

11) If you won the lottery, what would you do with the money?

If it's really a big amount of money, I would donate half of my winnings to a charity for sick and special children. I'd spend one-fourth on the personal needs of my family. I'd invest the remaining one-fourth of my winnings in trust funds, commercial papers or other forms of investments.

12) A calamity has hit your place, what would you do first? Should you evacuate the children? Decide your roles in the situation.

It depends on what type of calamity. If it's an earthquake and you're indoors, you are not supposed to go outside. In an earthquake, I'd gather the children inside and instruct them to take cover under a sturdy table, desk, or bench and other heavy

furniture. If we were outside, I would gather the children in an open area away from power lines, lampposts, high buildings and trees until the shaking stops.

13) If you were pregnant and you could choose the gender of your baby, what gender would you prefer? Give some specific reasons.

If it's my first baby, I'd prefer it to be a boy. I'd like my first born to be a boy because if anything happens to his parents, he would become the head of the family.

14) Who among the following will you choose: a rich person, someone who has good impression, a smart person, or a healthy person?

I'd choose a smart person. Because he is smart, he has the opportunities to become rich. Because he is smart, he would eat right and exercise to maintain his health. And because he is smart, he would make a good impression.

15) If your boyfriend had another girlfriend, what would you do?

I won't fight him, definitely, because that is not my style. Instead, I would talk to my boyfriend and ask him if what I found out was true. If he confirms it, then I'd tell him our relationship is over. If he doesn't, I'd give him the benefit of the doubt but remind him that there are three other things for a relationship to really work. These are trust, faithfulness and honesty.

16) If there is a shipwreck, what is the first thing you must do?

I'd see if my cell phone is still working and call for help. Then I'd check who and where the other survivors are.

17) If there is a thing you never want to lend to others, what is that and why?

I'd never lend my undergarments. Those items are very personal. It's very unhygienic to lend them to somebody else.

Transcript of a GROUP INTERVIEW

(Interviewer & Applicant A, B, C)

Interviewer: Now, you probably know that this interview is mostly to test your presence of mind in English. First, please tell us about what you are interested in recently from the person with lower application number.

A: I'm interested in abnormal weather and climatic changes, which are increasing recently. Experts say that the destruction of ozone layer is progressing due to the increase of such things as Freon or Halogen. So, I think all of us have to cooperate in handling this problem on a global basis.

Interviewer: Next, B, please.

B: I'm interested in music.

Interviewer: What type of music are you interested in?

B: Mainly in baroque music.

Interviewer: What is the baroque music? Please explain it in a little more detail.

B: It's not as heavy as classical or romantic music. I feel it is more expressive and colorful. It includes music from Bach to Handel.

Interviewer: It's your turn C, please.

C: I am interested in the news about earthquakes. We hear news about big earthquakes abroad frequently, and we also hear that we may have them. This is why I feel somewhat scared.

Interviewer: Please tell us just one thing you know about our company from

the person with application number 1.

A: Your head office is located in Houston.

B: You were established in July 1966.

C: You started your operations in Korea in October 1991.

Airline Cabin crew English
Intensive JOB INTERVIEW Training Module

Copyright ⓒ 2018 by **Kim, Chong Wook**

Printed in Korea
First : March 16. 2018
Publication : March 23. 2018

Publisher : Jung-Tae Park
ISBN : 978-89-7093-893-6 93740
Price : 20,000won

Kwangmoonkag Publishing Co.
161, Gwanginsa-gil, Paju Book City, Paju-si, Gyeonggi-do, Korea
Phone : +82-31-955-8787
Fax : +82-31-955-3730
E-mail : kwangmk7@hanmail.net
www.kwangmoonkag.co.kr